Written by Pamela Hickman • Illustrated by Heather Collins

STARTING WITH NATURE

STARTING WITH NATURE

Tree

BOOK

Kids Can Press

Published in Canada by
Kids Can Press Ltd.
29 Birch Avenue
Toronto, ON M4V 1E2

Published in the U.S. by
Kids Can Press Ltd.
85 River Rock Drive, Suite 202
Buffalo, NY 14207

Edited by Trudee Romanek
Series editor: Laurie Wark
Designed by Blair Kerrigan/Glyphics
Printed in Hong Kong by
Wing King Tong Company Limted

US 99 0 9 8 7 6 5 4 3 2 1
US PA 99 0 9 8 7 6 5 4 3 2 1

Canadian Cataloguing in Publication Data

Hickman, Pamela
        Starting with nature tree book

(Starting with nature series)
Includes index.
ISBN 1-55074-485-2 (bound) ISBN 1-55074-655-3 (pbk.)

1. Trees — United States — Juvenile literature. I. Collins, Heather.
II. Series: Hickman, Pamela. Starting with nature series.

QK115.H52 1998   j582.16'0973   C98-932152-5

Acknowledgments

Many thanks to my editors, Laurie Wark and Trudee Romanek, to Lori Burwash for coordinating so many schedules, and to our book designer, Blair Kerrigan. Thanks also to my family for their enthusiasm throughout our adventures in making maple syrup.

*For James,
Catherine and
Rebecca Hunter*
PH

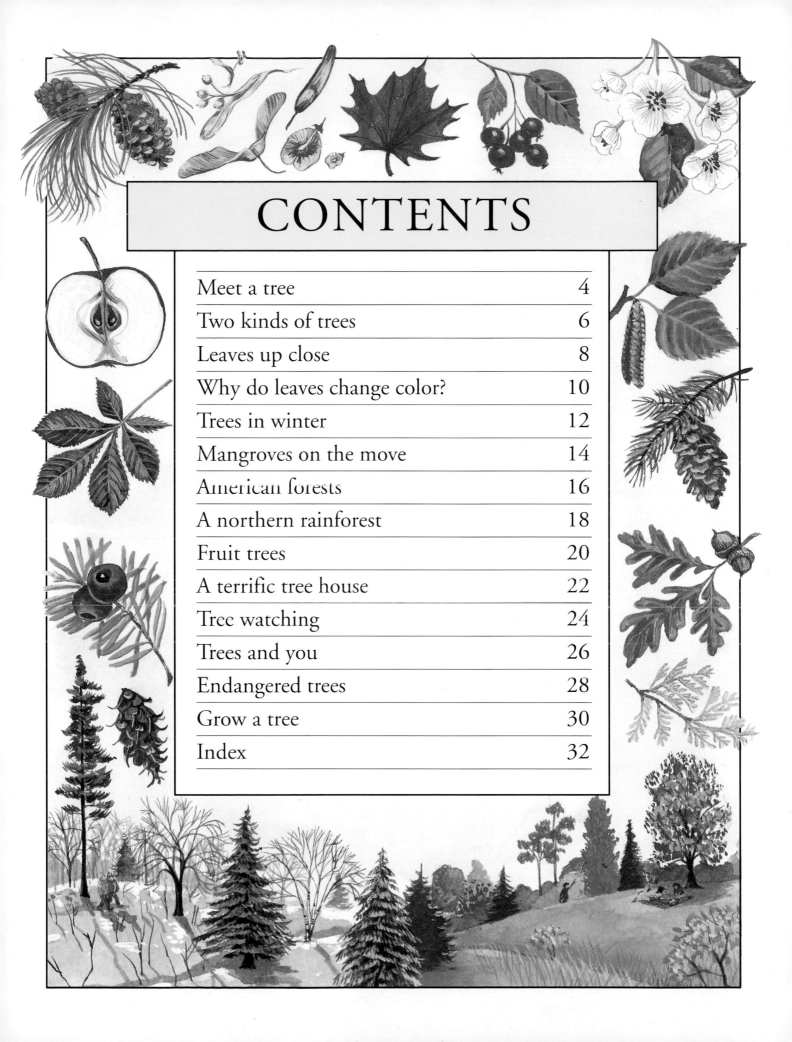

CONTENTS

Meet a tree

Do you like to climb trees, sit under their shady branches on a hot summer's day, eat apples and peaches, read books or watch birds? If you said yes to any of these, then trees are already an important part of your life. The United States is one of the most forested countries in the world. Trees provide food and shelter for wildlife, they help to keep the soil, water and air healthy, and their wood is used for lumber and paper. Whether you live in a forest in Oregon, a city in Pennsylvania or on the prairie grassland, you depend on trees every day. North America (excluding Mexico) has over 860 native tree species. Many kinds of trees from other parts of the world are planted in gardens and parks, too.

Take a look at the trees on these pages and discover how different kinds of trees from coast to coast have lots in common.

a trunk of wood protected by a covering of bark

roots to suck up water and minerals from the soil

leaves to make
food for the tree

all trees
produce
seeds

branches

Two kinds of trees

Have you ever noticed that some trees lose all their leaves at once, but other trees stay green all year around? Trees that lose their broad leaves in the fall or at the beginning of the dry season and grow a new set in the spring are called deciduous. Oaks and birches are deciduous trees. Coniferous trees, or conifers, such as pine and spruce, shed their old leaves, or needles, too. But they lose only a few at a time and new needles grow in before all the old ones fall off.

In the spring, deciduous trees have flowers. When the flowers are pollinated they produce seeds, which are often inside a fruit such as an apple or a beech nut. Conifers have cones instead of flowers. They produce seeds, but no fruit.

White Pine

White Oak

Two in one

Larch trees are two kinds of trees at once. They are coniferous because they have cones instead of flowers. But they are also deciduous, since they lose all of their needles in the fall and grow new ones the next spring.

OPEN AND CLOSE SESAME

After a forest fire, Jack Pines are the first trees to start growing. That's because their cones are opened by the heat of the fire and the seeds are released. After the fire, Jack Pine seeds are ready to grow on the newly burned ground, without competing with other plants for space.

White Pine cones have light dry seeds so that the wind can blow them to new places to grow. Their cones close up when it rains to keep the seeds dry. The cones open again on sunny days so the ripe seeds can be blown away. You can watch cones in action with this simple experiment.

You'll need:

2 Jack Pine or Scotch Pine cones

a cookie sheet

an oven

2 dry White Pine or hemlock cones with open scales

a large bowl of water

paper towel

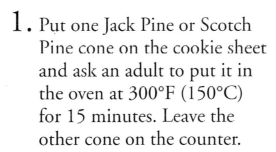

Jack Pine

Scotch Pine

hemlock

White Pine

1. Put one Jack Pine or Scotch Pine cone on the cookie sheet and ask an adult to put it in the oven at 300°F (150°C) for 15 minutes. Leave the other cone on the counter.

2. Compare the heated cone to the one on the counter.

3. Place a White Pine or hemlock cone in the bowl of water for 15 minutes. Leave the other cone on the counter for comparison.

4. Compare the wet and dry cones. Place the wet cone on a paper towel and let it dry. What happens to the cone as it dries?

Leaves up close

Look at the trees in your neighborhood. What color are their leaves? Most trees have green leaves because they are filled with a chemical called chlorophyll (say clor-o-fil). Chlorophyll helps the leaves make food to keep the trees healthy and to help them grow. The chlorophyll in the leaves uses energy from the sun, water from the soil and carbon dioxide from the air to make sugars, or glucose, to feed the trees. This process is called photosynthesis.

Leaves come in all different shapes and sizes. Some leaves are whole, or undivided, like a sycamore, and they are called simple leaves. Others, such as sumac leaves, are divided into tiny parts called leaflets. A sumac leaf is a kind of compound leaf.

Check out the leaves in your yard or local park. Can you find some simple leaves and some compound leaves? Look for leaves that have smooth edges and others that have little teeth along their edges. Leaves are important clues to helping you identify trees.

White Birch

Pacific Willow

American Sycamore

hickory

Linden

sumac

Mesquite

Red Oak

Make a leaf collection

You can gather green leaves in the summer and colorful leaves in the fall to make a collection. Collect as many different kinds of leaves as you can find on the ground. Glue or tape your leaves onto sheets of three-ringed paper. Beside each leaf, write where you found it, the date and what kind of tree it came from, if you know. Cover each sheet with clear plastic wrap and store the sheets in a binder.

You can make your leaves last longer by waxing them before you attach them to the paper. To wax leaves, place them between two sheets of waxed paper. Lay a cloth over the top sheet and ask an adult to press your leaves with a hot iron. The heat from the iron will melt the wax onto the leaves. The wax coating will keep your leaves from drying out or fading.

Why do leaves change color?

When the summertime greens of deciduous leaves turn to the reds, yellows, oranges and purples of fall, you know that winter is coming. Have you ever wondered where the bright autumn colors come from? The yellows and oranges are actually in the leaves all summer long, but they are hidden by the stronger green color of chlorophyll. When fall comes, leaves stop making chlorophyll. Soon afterward the green color disappears and the other colors take over.

HIDDEN COLORS

You can find the hidden colors in green leaves with this simple activity.

You'll need:

| some green leaves |
| a wide-mouth jar |
| rubbing alcohol |
| a spoon |
| scissors |
| a coffee filter |
| tape |
| a pencil |

1. Tear the leaves into little bits and put them in the jar with enough rubbing alcohol to cover them.
Caution: rubbing alcohol is poisonous. Ask an adult for help when using it.

2. Stir the mixture and then leave it for about five minutes. Colors from the leaves will dissolve in the rubbing alcohol.

3. Cut a strip 1½ in. (4 cm) wide and 3½ in. (9 cm) long from your coffee filter. Tape one end to the middle of your pencil.

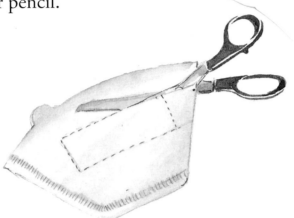

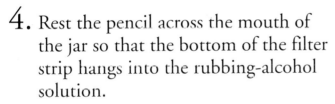

4. Rest the pencil across the mouth of the jar so that the bottom of the filter strip hangs into the rubbing-alcohol solution.

5. Watch as the filter strip soaks up the solution. When the filter paper is wet nearly to the top, lift it out of the jar and lay it on some paper to dry.

6. When the filter paper is dry, you will see different bands of color, which represent the colors in the leaves. Look for green, orange and yellow.

7. Try this activity with colorful fall leaves. Do you see a green band on your filter paper?

Trees in winter

In cold climates, some animals hibernate during winter to save energy and to avoid freezing. Trees also rest in the winter and stop growing. In the warm weather, the leaves of deciduous trees use a lot of water to make food for the tree. As long as there is enough water in the soil, the tree stays healthy. But in the winter when the ground is frozen, the tree can't get any water. To survive, the tree must stop water from being lost through the leaves, so a thin layer, like a scab, grows between the tree branch and the leaf. Each leaf is cut off from the tree's supply of water and minerals and eventually falls off the tree. In warmer climates, deciduous trees drop their leaves at the beginning of the dry season to conserve water.

scab

Take a look at a deciduous tree in winter. Its bare branches and grayish brown or white bark almost make the tree look dead. If you take a close-up look at the branches and twigs, though, you will see tiny buds at their tips and along their sides. These buds are like little packages, packed full of next spring's beautiful leaves and flowers. Check out the twigs of different trees and you'll find that buds come in all sorts of shapes, sizes and textures. Many buds are sticky with a waterproof resin that keeps the leaves inside warm and dry.

A big, old oak tree may drop 700 000 leaves in the fall. How long would it take you to rake all of them up?

Peek into a bud

In late winter or early spring, find a few different buds, the larger the better. Peel away the outer bud scales with your fingers or some tweezers. Inside the bud you will find the tiny, folded-up beginnings of the new leaves of spring. When the ground thaws in spring and the tree roots can suck up lots of water again, the buds begin to swell and grow as they take on water. Eventually the buds burst out of their coverings, and the tiny, pale, yellowish green leaves unfold and grow.

Mangroves on the move

If you travel to the Florida Keys in the southern part of Everglades National Park, you'll discover the amazing Red Mangrove trees along the ocean shore. Their leglike roots make mangroves look as if they are walking out to sea. Although they can't actually walk, mangroves do spread into nearby shallow water and, over the years, they help extend the shore further out to sea. Read on to find out how they do it.

ISLAND MAKERS

Follow this mangrove on the move and watch it create an island in the shallow sea.

1. A mangrove's seeds germinate, or begin to grow, while they are still attached to the tree. When the seedling is about one foot long it drops off the tree into the salt water.

2. The seedling is carried by water currents until it catches on a sandbar or coral reef under the shallow water. Roots grow quickly to help the seedling hang on.

3. Special prop roots grow out of the trunk to help hold the seedling in place. Sand, dead leaves and other materials in the water are trapped in the roots. Other mangrove seedlings become caught and begin to grow, too. After several years the pile of trapped material shows above water, like a small island.

4. As more sand and material is trapped, the water between the island and mainland becomes so shallow that other plants take root. Eventually the island connects to the mainland and becomes part of the expanding shore.

5. Mangroves not only create new land, but they also make very important habitats for shore birds such as egrets, spoonbills, herons, pelicans and storks.

Trees with knees

Have you ever heard of a tree with knees? Some trees that grow with their roots underwater all of the time, like mangroves, send up special "breathing roots" that poke above the mud at low tide. These roots, or knees, can take in oxygen from the air and send it down to the buried roots so the tree can breathe.

American forests

If you were walking through a forest on the west coast of Washington, you would see different trees than someone hiking in a forest in Alabama. That's because each kind of tree needs its own special combination of soil and climate to grow well. Look at the map to find out what forest regions are found in your state.

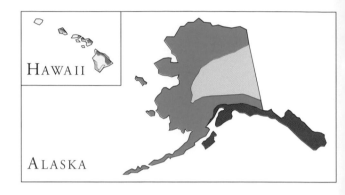

You can see on the map that not everyone in the United States lives in a forest area. People in parts of California, Nevada and Arizona may live in the dry scrub lands. Those who live in the central U.S. may live in the grasslands. Part of the land in Alaska is tundra, a wet, treeless area.

The place where the boreal forest stops growing and the tundra begins is called the tree line. Here the soils are too poor and the temperatures are too cold for trees to grow well. Another tree line is found in the mountains. The lower parts of the mountain slopes are often covered with trees, but higher up the soil is too thin and the winds are too strong and cold for trees to survive.

Forest Regions	Main Tree Species
Northern	Eastern White, Jack and Red Pines, Eastern Hemlock, Yellow Birch, Sugar Maple, American Beech
Southeastern	Shortleaf, Slash and Loblolly Pines, oak, magnolia, hickory
Central Hardwood	Black Walnut, American Sycamore, oak, maple, ash, sweetgum
Rocky Mountain	Lodgepole and Ponderosa Pines, Engelmann Spruce, Douglas Fir, Quaking Aspen
Pacific Coast	Douglas Fir, Western and Mountain Hemlock, cedar, pine, Western Larch, oak, Bigleaf Maple, Quaking Aspen
Subtropical	mangroves, West Indies mahogany, palms, Sapodilla

Hawaii Forests

Native forests   Mixed forests   Grasslands and volcanic areas

Other Regions

Tundra
Grasslands
Desert
Desert scrub and grass

A northern rainforest

When you hear the word "rainforest" you may think of steamy, hot jungles near the equator, but did you know that the northwest coast of the United States has its own kind of rainforest? The coastal forests of Alaska, Washington, Oregon and northern California have a temperate climate — it is very wet and mild — so plants can grow very large there. In fact, some of the largest trees in the U.S. grow in the temperate rainforest. Some trees are over 1000 years old and are as tall as a 30-story building!

If you walked into the rainforest and looked up, you would see huge Douglas Fir, Western Hemlock, Sitka Spruce and Western Red Cedar. If you looked down, you'd find the forest floor thickly covered with mosses, ferns and fungi. The rainforest is a wonderful habitat for wildlife, too, from the magnificent Roosevelt Elk to the yellow-and-black banana slug.

Some of the rainforest habitat is protected in parks, such as the Olympic National Park in Washington, but much of it is being destroyed by logging. In Oregon, over 90 percent of the original forests have been destroyed. New trees are planted to replace the ones that are cut down, but it takes many hundreds of years to form a rainforest habitat. Even if a new rainforest is allowed to grow, it will never be the same as the one that was destroyed. This is why many people across the country and around the world are asking the American governments to save more temperate rainforest before it's too late.

Bigleaf

Bigleaf Maples get their name from their enormous leaves. They are the largest leaves of any maple trees in America and can grow longer than this page. A Bigleaf's bark is special, too. It soaks up water so it is always damp, and this makes a great place for ferns, mosses and liverworts to grow.

Fruit trees

Juicy oranges and grapefruit, crisp apples and sweet plums are just some of the tasty treats that grow in orchards across the country. The United States has some of the best orchard-growing land in the world.

Pink and white blossoms fill the orchards with sweet perfume and attract thousands of honeybees. When the bees visit each flower to drink nectar and collect pollen for food, their hairy bodies become covered with pollen. When they visit the next flower, some of the pollen drops off and pollinates it. Once the flower has been pollinated, seeds begin to develop inside a thick, soft covering called a fruit. The fruit protects the seeds while they are developing, and it also attracts wildlife that eat the fruit and spread the seeds in their droppings.

Two of the best fruit-growing areas in the U.S. are southern California and Florida. The next time you go to the grocery store or local market, look to see how many of the fruits for sale were grown in these regions.

DRY SOME FRUIT SNACKS

You can dry some apples or pears in the fall and have delicious fruit snacks all winter long. Dried fruits make great snacks for hikes and camping trips, too.

You'll need:

some fresh apples and pears

an apple peeler

a knife

two cookie sheets

an oven

plastic bags

twist ties

1. Ask an adult to help you peel, core and thinly slice a few apples and pears.

2. Lay the fruit slices flat on the cookie sheets so that the slices do not overlap.

3. Have an adult preheat the oven to 200°F (100°C). Turn the oven off and place the cookie sheets in the oven for several hours. Reheat the oven every hour or so. When the fruit looks wrinkled, turn the slices over and dry them for a few more hours.

4. When the fruit looks and feels dry, put snack-size servings into small plastic bags and tie them tightly with twist ties. This keeps moisture from getting back into your fruit. Store the fruit in a cool, dry place.

If you have a fireplace or wood stove, you can dry some fruit the way your grandparents might have done it when they were kids. Thread your fruit slices on a string using a large darning needle. Ask an adult to hang the string of fruit from the mantle where the heat from the fire will dry the fruit quickly.

A terrific tree house

Trees make terrific homes for many animals, from tiny insects to Pine Martens and Great Blue Herons. All kinds of different animals may share one tree, using it for food, shelter and a place to raise their young. Birds often nest in tree holes or build their nests in the branches of trees. They feed on the tree's fruits and seeds, or on the insects that also live in the trees. Trees provide perches where birds can rest, as well as shelter from the cold and snow in winter. In this picture you'll see several tree-loving birds, as well as other animals that depend on trees for their survival. The next time you are out for a walk in the woods, see how many animals you can find at home in the trees.

Tree house trivia

Did you know . . .

. . . the Red-breasted Nuthatch smears a ring of sticky resin from pine trees around the entrance to its nesting cavity, possibly to keep out intruders?

. . . some ducks are born high up in trees? Wood Ducks, Buffleheads, Common Goldeneyes and Hooded and Common Mergansers all nest in tree cavities.

. . . Hairy Woodpeckers often carve out their nesting holes below a shelf of fungus growing on a tree trunk? The fungus works as an awning to shelter the nest.

Tree watching

Trees of all shapes and sizes grow throughout most of the United States. Tree watching is a great, year-round hobby no matter where you live. Choose a tree in your neighborhood and watch it throughout the seasons. Deciduous trees show more changes during the year than conifers. Draw pictures or take photos of the tree when it flowers in spring, spreads its green leaves in summer, drops its colorful leaves in fall, and stands bare and cold in winter. Using the checklist on these pages and a good field guide to trees, you can learn to identify your tree and others that you see.

Tree watching checklist

Leaves

Are the leaves needlelike or scalelike?

Are the leaves broad and flat?

Are they simple or compound?

What shape are the leaves?

Are there teeth along the edges of the leaves?

Are the leaves hairy or smooth?

Are the leaves growing opposite each other on the twig or are they arranged alternately?

What color are the leaves in the summer and the fall?

Flowers and fruit

Does the tree have flowers or cones?

If it has cones, what shape and size are they?
Do they grow at the top of the tree or
from the tips of the branches?

What color, shape and size are the flowers?

When ripe, is the fruit hard like a nut or
soft like a berry? What color is it?

What shape, size and color are the seeds?

Bark

Is the bark rough or smooth?

Is it scaly, stringy, flaky, peeling or ridged?

What color is the bark?

Buds

Are the buds pointed or rounded?

Are they sticky or dry?

Do the buds smell?

How are the buds arranged on the twig,
opposite or alternate?

Silhouettes

What is the general shape of the tree?

Is it wider at the top or the bottom?

Is it pointed or rounded at the top?

Does it have branches all the way down its
trunk or only partway down?

Trees and you

Look around your home and try to count all of the things that are made from trees. Include food, wood and paper products. Now imagine your home without any tree products. Trees and their products are part of our lives every day.

Trees are even more important in nature. They provide homes and food for wildlife. Their leaves and branches supply cooling shade and shelter from harsh winds. Tree roots hold onto the soil to keep it from being washed away. And during photosynthesis, trees take in carbon dioxide from the air and give off oxygen that wildlife and people need to breathe.

Tree talk

Trees don't have to talk to tell you about themselves. You can discover how old a tree was when it was cut down, or how much it grew in the last few seasons, just by looking at it closely.

If you find an old tree stump in the woods, examine the cut end. Wet the wood a bit and you'll see a pattern of light and dark rings. The light rings show the fast spring and early summer growth of the tree. The dark rings show the slower growth of late summer and early fall. Each pair of light and dark rings counts for one year of growth. Starting at the center of the stump, count the pairs of rings. This will tell you how old the tree was when it was cut.

spring and early
summer growth

bark

Winter is a great time to look at the twigs of deciduous trees, since they are bare and easy to see. Find a bumpy ring around a twig, close to the tip. This marks the beginning of last year's growth. The distance from this ring to the tip of the twig tells you how much the twig grew last spring and summer. You can keep track of how well the trees in your yard or neighborhood are growing by checking their twigs each winter. Which kind of tree is the fastest grower in your area? Which is the slowest?

late summer and early fall growth

AMERICA'S STATE TREES

Alabama	Southern (longleaf) Pine
Alaska	Sitka Spruce
Arizona	Paloverde
Arkansas	Pine
California	California Redwood
Colorado	Colorado Blue Spruce
Connecticut	White Oak
Delaware	American Holly
Florida	Sabal Palmetto
Georgia	Live Oak
Hawaii	Candlenut
Idaho	Western White Pine
Illinois	White Oak
Indiana	Tulip-tree (yellow poplar)
Iowa	Oak
Kansas	Cottonwood
Kentucky	Kentucky Coffee Tree
Louisiana	Bald Cypress
Maine	Eastern White Pine
Maryland	White Oak
Massachusetts	American Elm
Michigan	White Pine
Minnesota	Red (Norway) Pine
Mississippi	Magnolia
Missouri	Dogwood
Montana	Ponderosa Pine
Nebraska	Cottonwood
Nevada	Single-leaf Piñon
New Hampshire	White Birch
New Jersey	Red Oak
New Mexico	Piñon
New York	Sugar Maple
North Carolina	Pine
North Dakota	American Elm
Ohio	Buckeye
Oklahoma	Redbud
Oregon	Douglas Fir
Pennsylvania	Hemlock
Rhode Island	Red Maple
South Carolina	Palmetto
South Dakota	Black Hills Spruce
Tennessee	Tulip Poplar
Texas	Pecan
Utah	Blue Spruce
Vermont	Sugar Maple
Virginia	Dogwood
Washington	Western Hemlock
West Virginia	Sugar Maple
Wisconsin	Sugar Maple
Wyoming	Cottonwood

Endangered trees

If an animal is in danger, it can sometimes run away or hide to keep safe. Trees can't protect themselves when they are attacked by insects or disease, cut down, or when their habitat is destroyed. Some trees in the United States, such as the Florida Torreya and the Virginia Round-Leaf Birch, are listed as endangered or threatened and may die out completely unless something is done to protect them.

What are the problems? Destruction of their habitat for logging, farming and construction of roads and houses is causing these trees to die. Fortunately, some trees are protected in parks and nature reserves. Conservation groups and local governments are also teaching local landowners about the need to protect the habitats of these species.

YOU CAN HELP

You can help to protect the trees in your neighborhood and across the country by telling your friends and family how important trees are in nature and in our lives. Read on to discover some ways to help trees.

1. Remind your friends never to pull bark off trees or to carve in it. The bark protects the tree from insects, fungi and disease that can hurt or kill the tree.

2. Ask your parents not to cut down trees on your property. Plant new trees if you have the space. Trees provide food and shelter for birds and other wildlife.

3. Write to your local town or city council and ask them to plant more trees along the streets or in the parks. Explain why trees are important.

4. Ask your teacher if your class can plant a tree at school and care for it. This is a good Arbor Day or Earth Day event.

5. Raise money for a conservation group that is working to protect trees in the United States. Have a sale of reusable tree products such as books, magazines and items made of wood.

6. Help to save trees by reducing, reusing and recycling tree products. Ask your parents to buy recycled paper products. Avoid using disposable plates, napkins and cups. Choose products with little or no packaging. Recycle newspapers, writing and computer paper and cardboard. Always write on both sides of paper.

Did you know that for every ton of recycled paper that is made, 17 trees are saved?

Grow a tree

You can grow a tree in your backyard or on a balcony by planting seeds. Why not plant a tree on your birthday or for someone else's special day to celebrate the event? Your gift may last a lifetime. Choose a place where the tree will have room to grow and won't be in the way of other activities in the yard. You can collect seeds from nearby trees or from locally grown fruit, or buy them at a garden center. Once your tree is planted, take care of it to make sure it survives. Watch how your tree grows and changes throughout the seasons and keep notes about the wildlife that visit it.

You'll need:

seeds from trees such as apple, horse chestnut, maple, peach or walnut

a shovel

compost (optional)

water

gravel and potting soil

a large, plastic flowerpot (optional)

1. If you are using local seeds, collect and plant them in the fall, or look for sprouted seeds on the ground in the spring. A sprouted seed is cracked with a tiny, white root coming out. It may also have two small, green leaves growing out of it. Check the ground for sprouted seeds near maples, horse chestnuts, elms, oaks and other trees that produce lots of seeds.

2. Dig a small hole in the ground where you want your tree to grow. Loosen the soil inside the hole to help the tree roots spread more easily. Put some compost in the hole and water it.

3. Gently place the seed in the hole and cover it with soil. If the seed has already sprouted, be careful not to break off the tiny root. Keep the green leaves above the soil.

4. A small garden fence or some branches laid around your seedling will help to keep people and pets from stepping on it.

5. If you are planting your seed in a pot, put gravel in the bottom of the pot for drainage before filling the pot with soil. Dig a small hole and fill it with water. Plant your seed in it and cover it with soil. Native trees should be left outside all winter.

6. As your tree grows bigger, it may need a tall wooden stake beside it to provide support for the trunk.

Index

A
age of a tree, 26

B
bark, 4, 13, 19, 29
birds, 22–23
buds, 13

C
chlorophyll, 8, 10–11
compound leaves, 8
cones, 6–7
coniferous trees, 6–7, 24
conservation, 18, 28–29

D
deciduous trees, 6–7, 24, 28
dry season, 6, 12

E
endangered trees, 18, 28–29

F
features of a tree, 4–5, 24–25
flowers, 6, 20
forest fires, 7
forest types of the United
    States, 16–17
fruit, 6, 20, 22
    drying, 21
fruit trees, 20–21

G
growing a tree, 30–31
growth of a tree, 18, 19
    measuring, 27

L
leaf collecting, 9
leaves, 5, 8–9, 14, 26
    colors of, 8, 10–11
    falling off, 6, 12
    inside a bud, 13
    shapes of, 8

M
mangrove trees, 14–15
maple trees, 19, 27

N
needles, 6

O
orchards, 20

P
people and trees, 4, 14, 20, 26
    See also endangered trees
photosynthesis, 8, 26
planting a tree, 30–31
pollination, 6, 20

R
rainforests, 18–19
roots, 4, 26

S
seeds, 5, 6–7, 20, 22, 30–31
simple leaves, 8
species in North America, 4
species in the United States,
    16–17
state trees, 27

T
trees in nature, 4, 14, 22–23,
    26
    See also wildlife and trees
tree line, 16–17
tree parts, 4–5, 24–25
tree products, 4, 20, 26, 29
tree rings, 26
tree watching, 24–25, 26–27,
    30

W
wildlife and trees, 4, 14, 18,
    20, 22–23, 26
winter, 12–13, 22, 27